Let's Sew

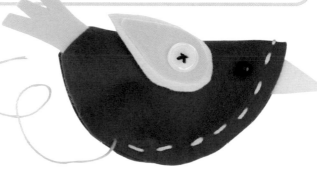

Penguin Random House

Senior designer **Hannah Moore**
Project editor **Anne Hildyard**
Photographer **Lynda Kelly**
Senior producer **Ché Creasey**
Producer, Pre-Production **Tony Phipps**
Jacket designer **Amy Keast**
Creative technical support **Sonia Charbonnier**
Managing editor **Penny Smith**
Managing art editor **Marianne Markham**
Art director **Jane Bull**
Publisher **Mary Ling**

First published in Great Britain in 2016 by
Dorling Kindersley Limited
80 Strand, London WC2R 0RL

A CIP catalogue record for this book
is available from the British Library.
ISBN: 978–0–2412–3101–2
Printed in China.
All images © Dorling Kindersley Limited
For further information see: www.dkimages.com

A WORLD OF IDEAS
SEE ALL THERE IS TO KNOW

www.dk.com

Contents

Let's learn to sew!

Introduction

To start sewing, the first thing you need is a needle and thread. Then you can learn how to put the thread through the needle, and how to make a knot at the end of the thread. Next come two basic stitches, running stitch and backstitch. After that, you will be able to use these stitches to make some of the lovely projects in the book. With just a little practice, the results will be perfect!

Getting started

At the beginning of each project is a list of everything you will need to make it. Then, with the help of an adult, gather together an essential sewing kit (see pages 6–7), and **start sewing!**

Take care with scissors and needles!

Sewing safety

All the projects in this book are to be made under adult supervision. Always take extra care when sharp implements such as scissors, sewing needles, or pins are used to make a project. **Always ask an adult to help you.**

Yes, we're made out of old socks!

Make **cool projects** from scraps of fabric, odd buttons, and even old socks!

Sewing kit

These are the things you will need to make the projects in the book.

Fur fabric
This is perfect for ears.

Bright fabric
This brings your animals to life. Pinking the edges stops them fraying.

Right side
of the fabric.

Wrong side
of the fabric.

Fleece fabric
This doesn't fray, and it is very easy to cut.

Felt
Scraps of bright felt are great as decorations.

Ribbons and cords
All of these are useful for bag straps, horses' reins, or for decoration.

6

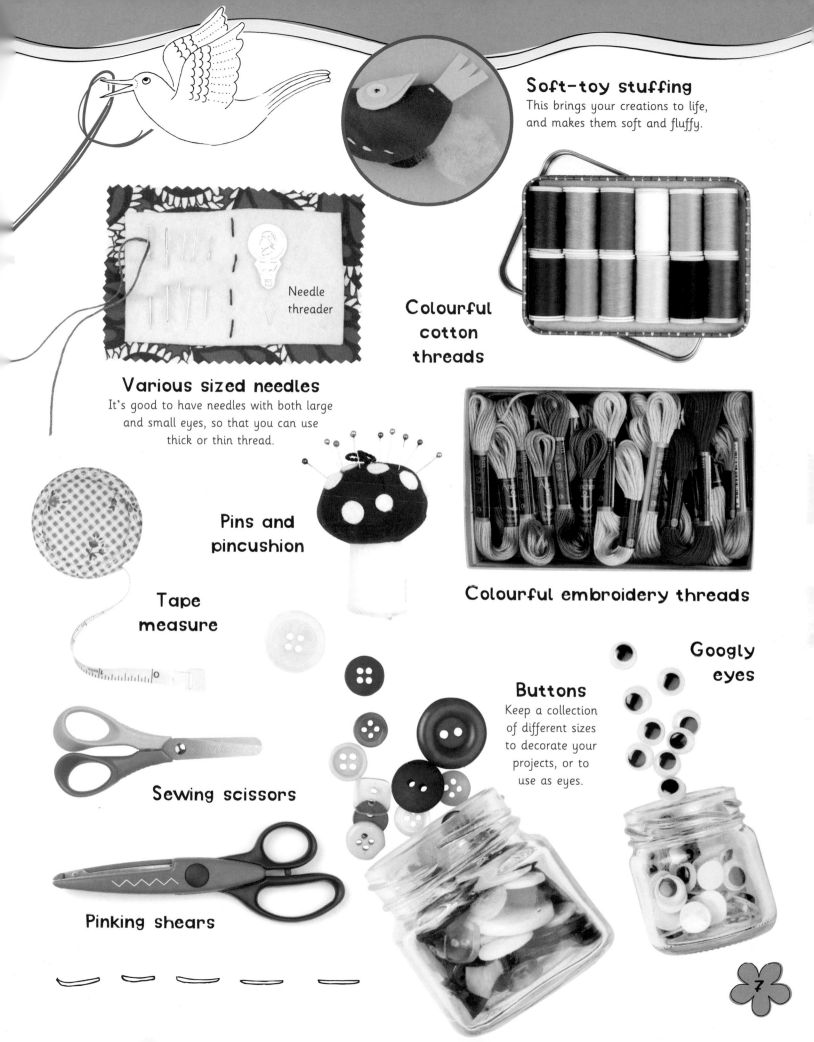

Soft-toy stuffing
This brings your creations to life, and makes them soft and fluffy.

Various sized needles
It's good to have needles with both large and small eyes, so that you can use thick or thin thread.

Needle threader

Colourful cotton threads

Colourful embroidery threads

Pins and pincushion

Tape measure

Sewing scissors

Pinking shears

Buttons
Keep a collection of different sizes to decorate your projects, or to use as eyes.

Googly eyes

7

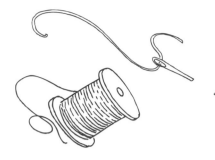

Threading a needle

Before you can start sewing, you need to **thread your needle**. Then you make a knot in the end of the thread. This is the very first step to sewing!

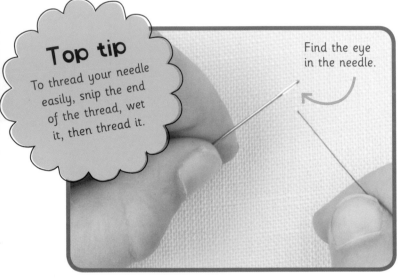

Find the eye in the needle.

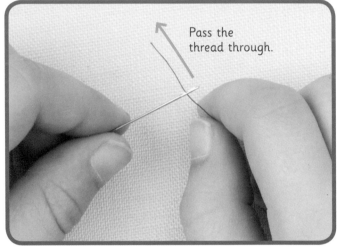

Pass the thread through.

 1 **Line up needle and thread**

Smooth the end of the thread. Hold the needle in one hand, and the end of the thread in the other.

 2 **Push thread through needle**

Slip the end of the thread through the eye of the needle. If the eye is big enough it should pass through easily.

Choose a needle that works with your thread.

Knot the longer end of the thread.

Using a needle threader

Too tricky?
If it's hard to thread your needle, try using a needle threader.

Needle threader

1 **Slip needle threader through needle**

Push the wire loop of the needle threader through the eye of your needle. Then put the thread through the wire loop.

Push through eye.

2 **Pull through the needle**

Pull the wire back through the needle, until the thread is brought through with it.

Pull threader out.

3 **Pull thread out of wire**

Remove the thread from the threader by sliding the wire loop off the thread.

Slide threader off.

4 **Tie a knot in the thread**

If you want to sew with a single thread, make a knot in the longest end. Then you can start sewing!

Now you're ready to sew!

9

Running stitch

You've threaded your needle – now it's time to make your first **stitch!** Running stitch is the easiest.

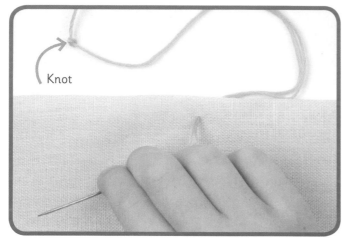

Knot

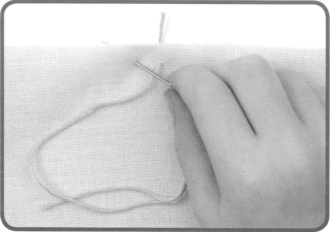

1 Sew the first stitch
Thread your needle and knot the end of the thread. Push the needle through the fabric, dragging the thread through to the other side until the knot stops it.

2 Up and down
One stitch length along, push the needle back through the fabric to the other side.

Running stitch in a contrast colour looks cool.

Finishing off

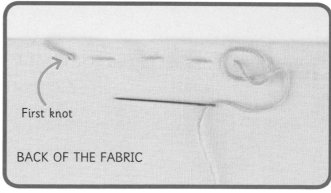

First knot

BACK OF THE FABRIC

1 Make a knot
To finish, make a knot at the end of your sewing by twisting the thread to make a loop, then pulling the needle through it.

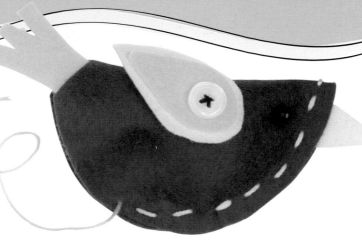

Join up!
Use running stitch to **sew two pieces** of fabric together, or to make a broken line.

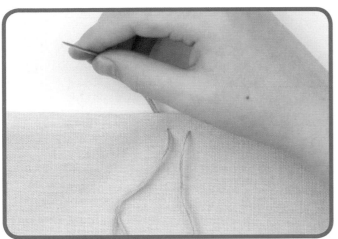

 3 **Pull the thread through**

Pull the thread all the way through to the other side of the fabric.

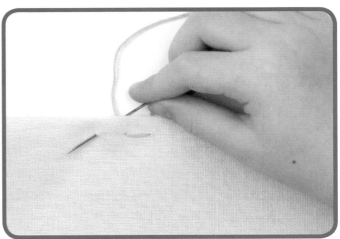

 4 **Back to the front**

Keeping the stitch the same size, push your needle to the front. Repeat to make more stitches.

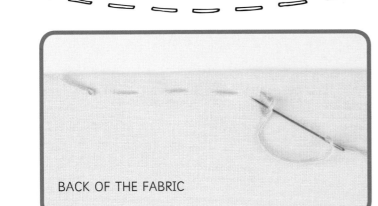

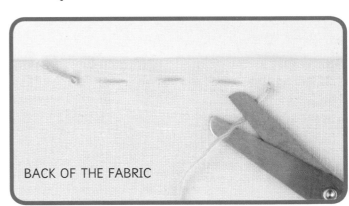

BACK OF THE FABRIC

BACK OF THE FABRIC

 2 **Finish off**

Make another loop, then push the needle through it again. Pull tight so that the knot sits close to the fabric.

 3 **Trim the thread**

Neaten the back of the fabric by snipping off the excess thread by the knot.

11

Backstitch

Backstitch is a strong stitch that makes a continuous line. It looks like stitches made on a sewing machine.

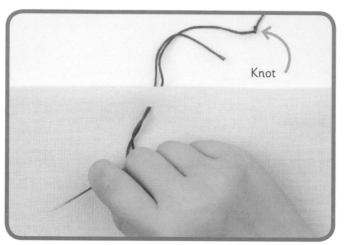

Knot

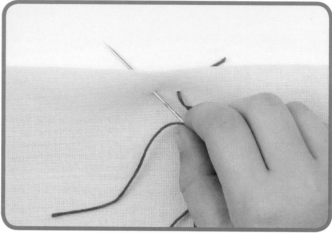

1 **Starting off**
Make a knot in your thread and push the needle up through the fabric to the front side.

2 **Make your first stitch**
Push your needle through to the back, one stitch length ahead of where your needle came out.

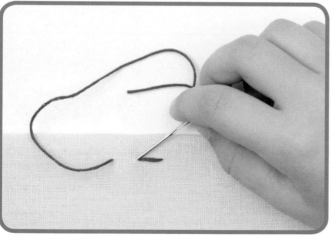

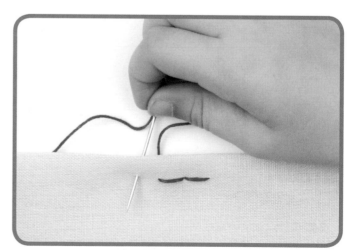

4 **Go backwards**
Bring the needle back to where the last stitch finished. Push the needle through to the back to make the stitch.

5 **Go forwards**
Bring the needle out one stitch length ahead of the last stitch.

12

Backstitch is one stitch back then one forward.

Wrong side

The stitches on the right side are **neat and even**, but they look quite messy on the wrong side.

Right side

3 Next stitch

Bring your needle through from the back, one stitch length ahead of where your needle went through.

Backstitch brings a **smile** to my face.

Buttons galore!

Great for fastenings and decoration, buttons also make perfect eyes for toys. First you have to learn to sew them on!

How to sew on a button

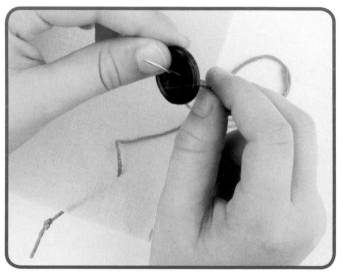

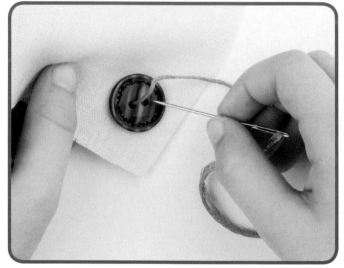

 1 **Pull the thread through**

Knot the thread, then push the threaded needle up through the fabric and one hole of the button. Pull the needle through so the button drops near the fabric.

 2 **Push to the other side**

Push the needle back through the other hole in the button, and then to the back of the fabric. Then bring the needle back through the fabric and the first hole.

Buttons will add a pop

Buttons come in all shapes and sizes.

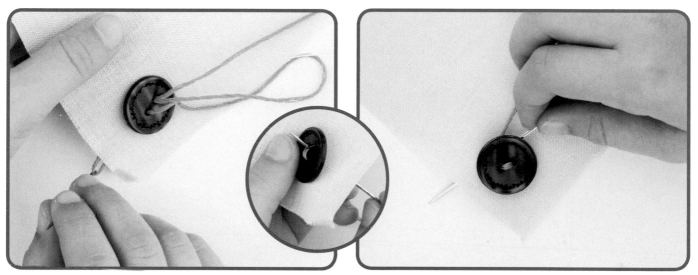

3 **Go over and over**
Keep stitching up and down through the button and fabric. Do this about 10 times so the button holds firmly.

4 **Finishing off**
To secure the button, bring the thread under the button. Sew backwards and forwards behind the button, then cut the thread.

of colour **to your sewing!**

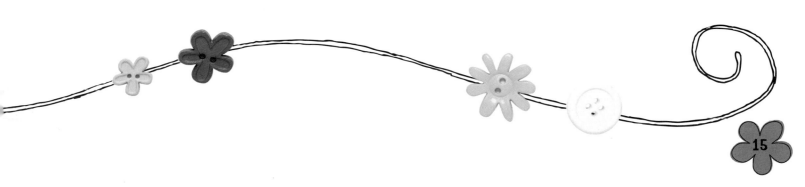

Sewing cards

Sew colourful stars, hearts, and swirly shapes onto bright backgrounds. They make **great** gifts or greetings cards for your friends and family.

Make them stand out!

Use bright thread that really stands out from the background card to create a bold look.

Use the **templates** on page 59 for this design, and for the other patterns.

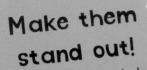

Sew a wavy pattern in **running stitch**, adding buttons as you go.

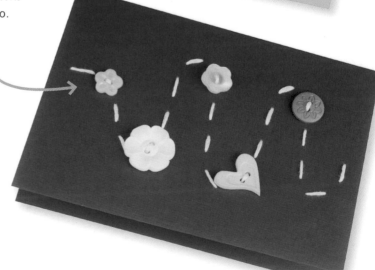

Top tip

Plan your designs on a piece of paper before you start making your cards.

You will need

- card • a piece of thick cardboard
- thin paper • pins
- embroidery thread • tapestry needle • buttons

How to make a card

Fold the card in half, then open it out again. Place it on a piece of thick cardboard.

1 ⭐ **Prick out the design**

Trace a design from page 59 onto paper or draw your own. Add dots to show where the stitches will go. Push a pin through the dots and the card.

2 ⭐ **Sew your design**

Thread a needle and tie a knot in the end. Pass the needle through a hole from the inside. Use backstitch, passing the needle through all the holes.

Top tip

Embroidery thread shows up well, since it is thicker than ordinary sewing thread.

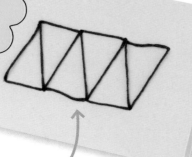

Simple **patterns** are fairly easy to make.

3 ⭐ **Finish your design**

Keep passing the needle through the holes until the design is finished. Pull the needle to the inside and knot the thread.

Bright and lively
Instead of making your elephants grey, make them in **lovely coloured felt or fleece**.

The elephant family is off on a trip. Do you think they'll go on a jumbo jet?

You will need

thin paper • felt • pins • scissors • pieces of fabric • tapestry needle and embroidery thread • soft-toy stuffing • yarn • googly eyes • fabric glue

Eddie the elephant

These adorable elephants are so easy to sew, you can make a whole family.

I need to pack my trunk for the big trip.

2 layers of felt

Body
cut 2

Ears
cut 2 fabric
cut 2 felt

⭐ 1 Make the template

Trace the templates on page 60 onto thin paper and cut them out. Pin the body shape onto two layers of felt and cut around the shape.

⭐ 2 Make the ears

Use the ear template to cut out two ears in fabric and two in felt. Pin each fabric ear to a felt ear and sew, leaving the flat edge open.

Make two ears.

1 layer of felt and 1 layer of fabric.

⭐ 5 Attach the tail, sew up, add eyes

With the tail in place, sew up the gap to close. Glue an eye on each side.

Cut a short piece of yarn for the tail and make a knot at the end.

Don't forget to add my googly eyes!

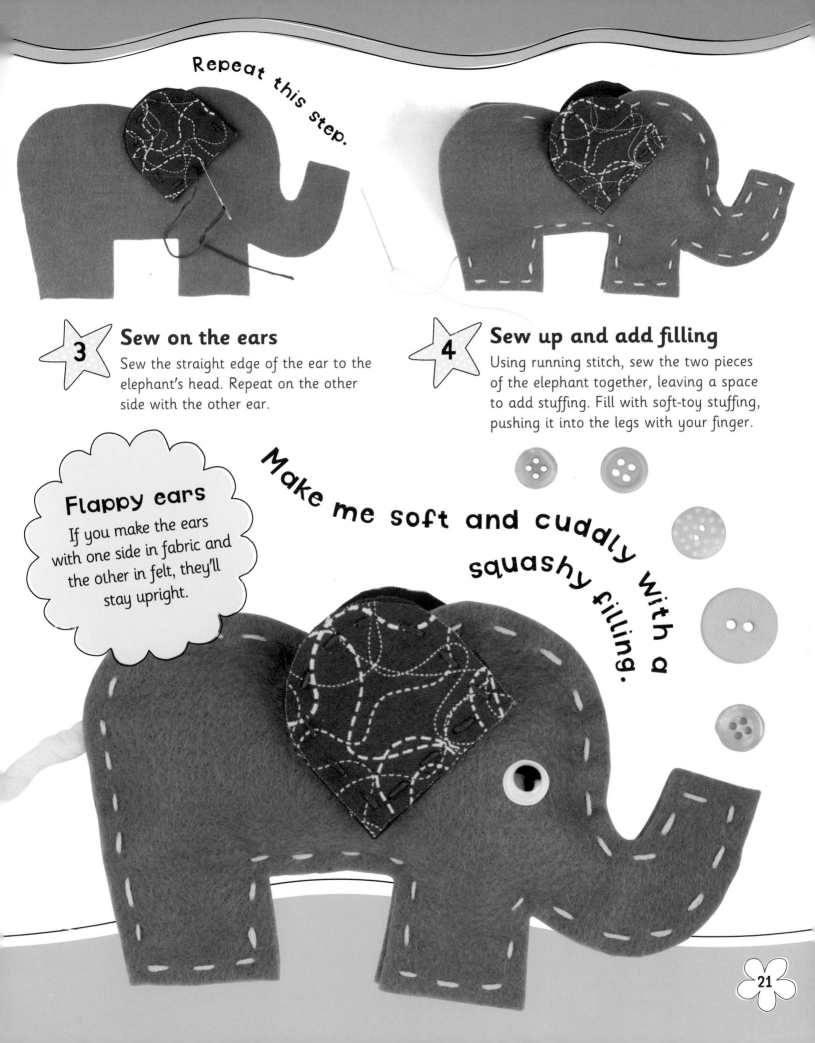

Repeat this step.

3 ⭐ Sew on the ears

Sew the straight edge of the ear to the elephant's head. Repeat on the other side with the other ear.

4 ⭐ Sew up and add filling

Using running stitch, sew the two pieces of the elephant together, leaving a space to add stuffing. Fill with soft-toy stuffing, pushing it into the legs with your finger.

Flappy ears

If you make the ears with one side in fabric and the other in felt, they'll stay upright.

Make me soft and cuddly with a squashy filling.

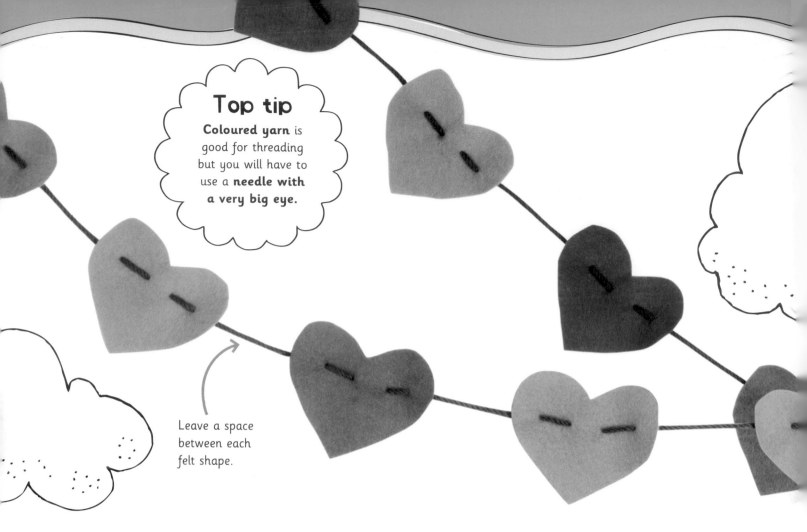

Top tip

Coloured yarn is good for threading but you will have to use a needle with a very big eye.

Leave a space between each felt shape.

Put the flags out!

Flags aren't just for outdoors – this cheerful bunting will brighten up any room. And all you need to do is thread a few simple felt shapes together!

You will need

thin paper · felt · tapestry needle · yarn or thin cord

Transform your room!

1 **Cut out the pieces**
Trace the template on page 58 onto thin paper and cut it out. Pin onto felt and cut out the shapes.

2 **Thread the shapes**
With a needle and yarn, thread the felt shapes together with a couple of running stitches in each.

Flower power

Charming colours

Dotty donkey

See who can design the most original bottle carrier. You can **create monsters**, animals, or just fun patterns.

You will need

socks • scissors • needle and thread • string or cord • thin paper • pins • felt • buttons • ribbon • scraps of fabric

It's hard to believe I used to be a sock!

24

Starry starry night

Recycle old socks...
...turn them into something new!

Stripes and spots

Bottle carriers

You'll always have a drink handy with these cheerful holders. Buy some colourful socks or use up your odd ones. With just a few tweaks you'll be ready to go!

Using the top-end

⭐ **1** **Cut off the foot**
Cut the sock just above the heel. You only need the top part of the sock for your carrier.

Top tip
Recycle any leftover socks. You can cut them into rings and use as cool hair bands.

The sock is inside out.

⭐ **2** **Sew the end**
Turn the sock inside out. Sew up the cut end of the sock using backstitch.

Using the toe-end

⭐ **1** **Make a decoration**
Trace the templates on page 62 onto thin paper and cut them out. Pin them onto felt and cut around the shapes.

⭐ **2** **Cut the top off the sock**
Cut the sock to the required size. Place the felt flower on the felt circle and sew on a button.

26

3 Add the handle

Cut a long piece of cord for the handle. Place each end on the inside of the sock. Sew lots of stitches over each other to hold the handle in place.

Keep hydrated!

Don't dry up! Take your bottle carrier with you and drink lots of water – especially when it's hot.

Top tip

You might find it easier to sew on the **trimming** if you put a bottle in your carrier first.

4 Add the handle

Pin each end of the handle to the sock. Sew lots of stitches over each other to hold the strap firmly in place.

3 Sew on decoration

Pin the ribbon to the cut edge, then sew it on using running stitch. Pin and sew the felt decoration to the sock.

27

Rainbow birdies

Wouldn't it be fun to make a brilliant birdie in every colour of the rainbow? The sky's the limit!

Take flight
To make your birds fly, hang them from a twig or branch.

You will need

thin paper • pins • scissors • felt • needle and thread • buttons • beads • tapestry needle and embroidery thread • soft-toy filling

29

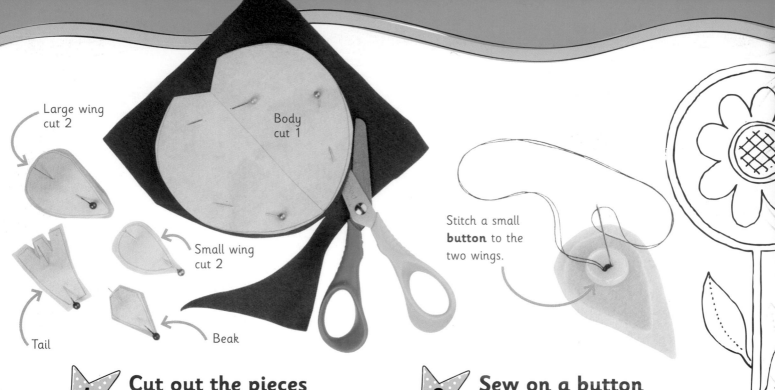

Large wing
cut 2

Body
cut 1

Small wing
cut 2

Tail

Beak

Stitch a small **button** to the two wings.

1 Cut out the pieces

Use the templates on page 60 to cut out a body, beak, wings, and tail from thin paper. Pin the templates onto felt and cut around them.

2 Sew on a button

Place each large wing together with a small wing and sew together through the button.

Put the tail in position before you sew.

Use **running stitch** around the edges.

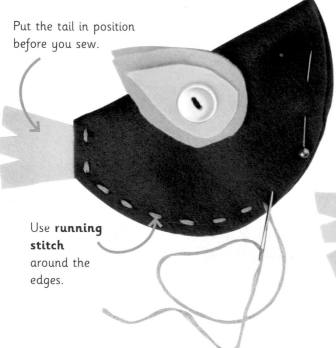

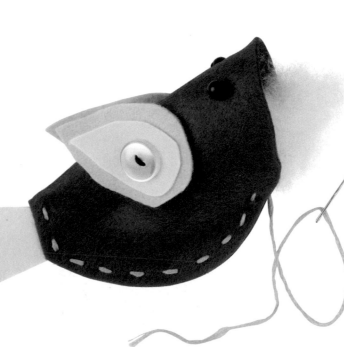

5 Pin and sew together

Fold the body in half. Pin, then sew the tail in place. Sew around the edge of the body, leaving a gap for the filling.

6 Add the filling

Stuff the bird with soft-toy filling. You can push it in with a pencil, or your finger if you prefer.

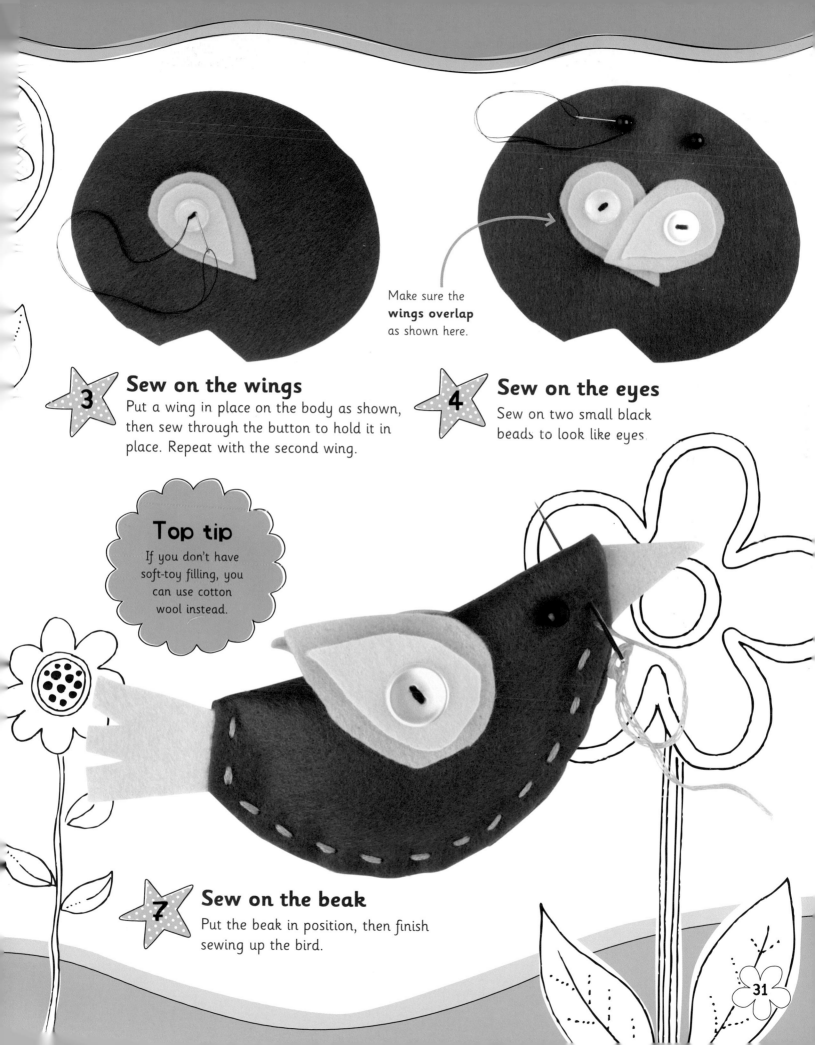

3 Sew on the wings

Put a wing in place on the body as shown, then sew through the button to hold it in place. Repeat with the second wing.

Make sure the **wings overlap** as shown here.

4 Sew on the eyes

Sew on two small black beads to look like eyes.

Top tip

If you don't have soft-toy filling, you can use cotton wool instead.

7 Sew on the beak

Put the beak in position, then finish sewing up the bird.

31

Wonderful whales

These swimming giants are having a whale of a time! Make them from soft, coloured fleece, then sew a lovely smile in a different colour.

Will you sing us a special whale song, please?

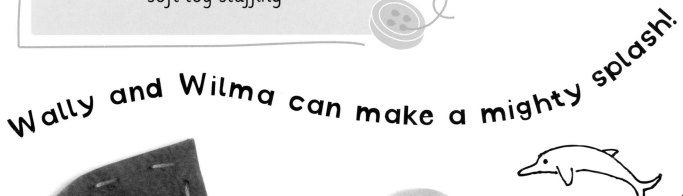

You will need

thin paper · scissors · fleece · tapestry needle and embroidery thread · buttons · soft-toy stuffing

Wally and Wilma can make a mighty splash!

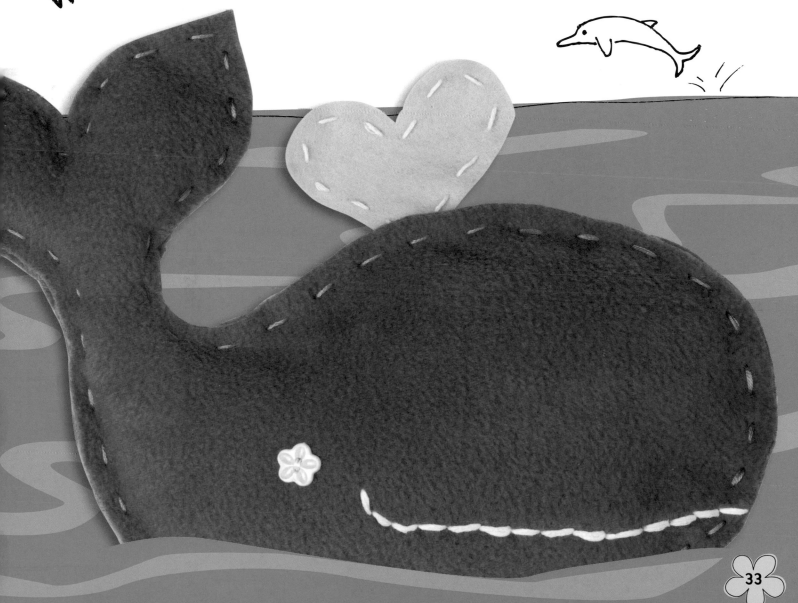

33

Two layers of fleece fabric

Copy the templates on page 61

Top tip

If you use two layers of fleece for the water jet, it's less likely to flop over. You could also add a bit of stuffing to make it a thicker shape.

Top tip

Fleece fabric is great because it's soft, cuddly, and it doesn't fray.

Two layers of fleece fabric

 Cut out the body

Copy the templates on page 61 onto thin paper. Cut and pin them onto two pieces of fleece, then cut out the shapes.

 Sew the water jet

Put the two pieces for the water jet together and sew together using running stitch. Add stuffing if you want to.

Attach the water jet.

5 **Sew up the whale**

Pin the water jet in position then start sewing up the whale using running stitch – but leave a gap at the front.

6 **Add the stuffing**

Push the soft-toy stuffing into the whale using a pencil or your finger to fill up the tail.

Repeat to put a **smile** on the other side of the face.

One layer of fleece fabric

One layer of fleece fabric

3 Sew the mouth

On each separate piece of the whale's face, draw a pencil line curving at one end. Then sew over it with backstitch.

4 Sew on the eyes

Sew a small button on one side of the whale so that it looks like an eye. Repeat on the opposite side.

Come and play with me — we can **ride the waves.**

7 Close up

Sew running stitch along the open end. Finish with a double stitch.

Make them
extra special

Add felt flowers, colourful buttons, or cut-out animals or shapes to make all your bags feel personal.

These bags are great for keeping your goodies safe!

Bags of fun!

Need a bag to keep all your odds and ends?
Here's how to sew a real original using your
very own design and favourite colours.

Make a home for tiny dinos.

You will need

pinking shears • different kinds
of fabric • pins • sewing needle
and thread • tapestry needle and
embroidery thread • yarn • ribbon

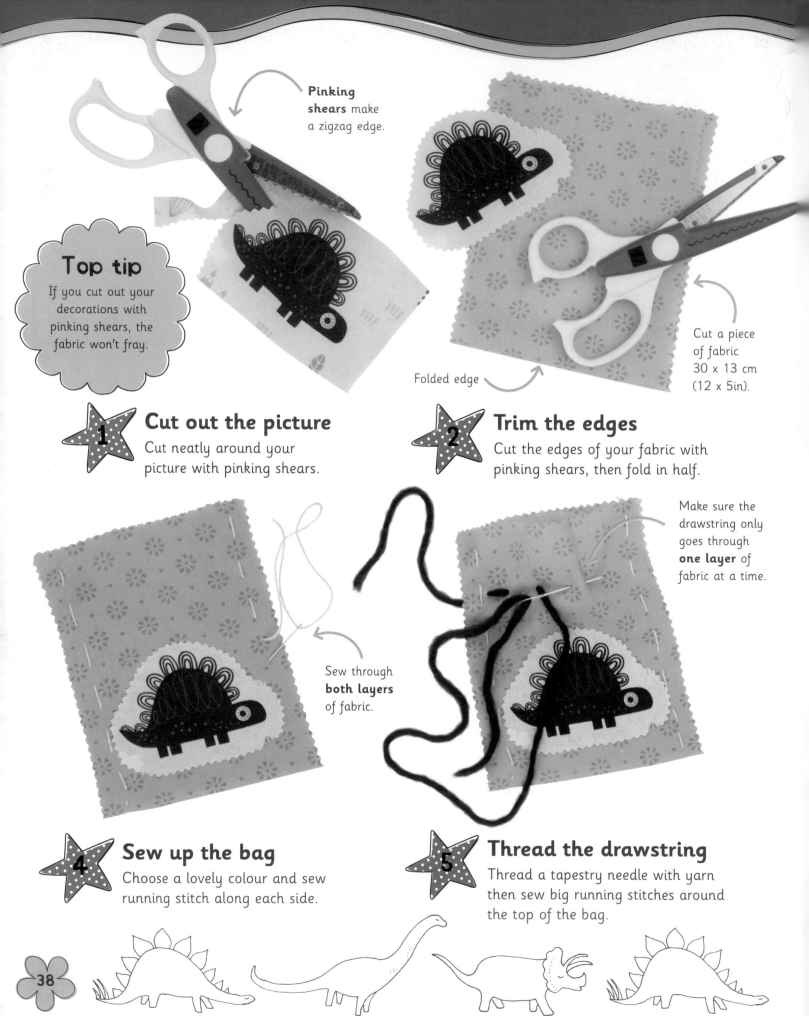

Pinking shears make a zigzag edge.

Top tip

If you cut out your decorations with pinking shears, the fabric won't fray.

Folded edge

Cut a piece of fabric 30 x 13 cm (12 x 5in).

1 Cut out the picture

Cut neatly around your picture with pinking shears.

2 Trim the edges

Cut the edges of your fabric with pinking shears, then fold in half.

Make sure the drawstring only goes through **one layer** of fabric at a time.

Sew through **both layers** of fabric.

4 Sew up the bag

Choose a lovely colour and sew running stitch along each side.

5 Thread the drawstring

Thread a tapestry needle with yarn then sew big running stitches around the top of the bag.

Top tip

Sew your dinosaur on just **one side** of the bag or you won't be able to open it!

Folded edge

Sew on the picture

Pin your picture to one side of the bag. Sew onto the bag with running stitch.

Gently **pull both ends of yarn** tightly to close the bag.

6 Tie a knot and close

Pull the drawstring through, then tie the ends together with a knot.

A hemmed bag

Sew up the hem

Cut a narrow rectangle for your bag. Fold over both the short ends to make a hem. Pin, then sew in place with running stitch.

2

Sew up the bag

Place both hems together. Sew up the long sides of the bag with running stitch.

3

Thread the ribbon

Thread a needle with ribbon. Push it through one hem then the other. Knot the ends of the ribbon.

That bag is just my colour.

I'm the star of the show!

You will need

thin paper • pins • scissors • felt • small buttons
• rickrack braid • ribbon • needle and sewing
threads • tapestry needle and embroidery thread
• soft-toy filling • googly eyes • fabric glue

Under the sea

Once you've made a few of these cute little fish, you can invent your own underwater world to fill with jellyfish, starfish, and all their friends.

Wait for me, my legs feel like jelly!

We love to splish and splash with our cool friends

How to make a fish

Mouth cut 1

Body cut 2

Eyes cut 2

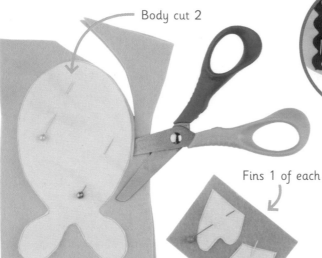

Fins 1 of each

Sew through the button to secure each eye.

1 Cut out the pieces

Trace the templates on page 62 onto thin paper. Cut them out and pin onto pieces of felt. Cut out the shapes.

2 Sew on the decoration

Sew on felt circles and buttons for eyes. Pin rickrack on each side of your fish and sew in place using running stitch.

Sew **both fins** on before stuffing

4 Add the filling

Use soft-toy filling to stuff the body. Push it into the tail with a pencil or a finger.

5 Add the mouth

Put the mouth in place, pin, and then sew up the rest of your fish.

How to make a jellyfish

 1 **Cut out the shapes**
Trace the template onto thin paper. Cut it out and pin it onto felt. Cut out two body shapes.

2 **Sew up and add the filling**
Sew the two pieces together around the edge. Add the filling to the open end.

 3 **Sew up the body**
Pin the two halves of the body together, put the fins in place, then sew part way around with running stitch.

Sew through each piece of rickrack to hold it in place.

Making friends
You can find templates at the back of the book to make me and the other fish. Why don't you make all of us? The more the merrier!

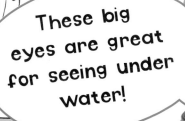

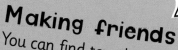

 3 **Position rickrack and sew up**
Put lengths of rickrack just inside the jellyfish body. Pin, then stitch to hold the rickrack in place.

 4 **Attach googly eyes**
Glue the eyes in position.

These big eyes are great for seeing under water!

My ears feel lovely and furry.

Barney bear bag

Everyone will want one of these adorable bags. As well as being so appealing, they're easy-peasy to make.

You can jazz me up with a coloured strap.

You will need

thin paper · felt · fur fabric · tapestry needle
and embroidery thread · needle and sewing
thread · buttons · cord or ribbon

45

Make Barney bear

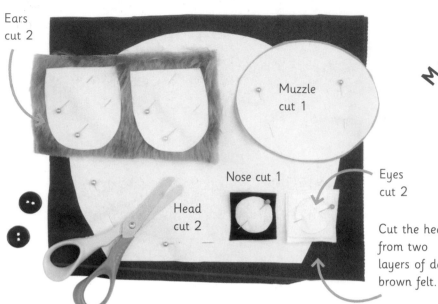

Ears
cut 2

Muzzle
cut 1

Nose cut 1

Head
cut 2

Eyes
cut 2

Cut the head
from two
layers of dark
brown felt.

Make Barney smile!

Draw a
faint pencil
line as a
guide for
his smile.

---

1 ### Cut out the pieces
Trace the templates on page 63 onto paper
and cut them out. Pin the head, muzzle,
eyes, and nose onto felt and pin the ears
onto fur fabric. Cut out all the shapes.

2 ### Sew the nose and mouth
Sew a nose onto the muzzle with
running stitch. For his mouth, stitch
over your pencil marks in backstitch.

Top tip
Sew lots of stitches
over each other to
hold the strap firmly
in place.

5 ### Sew the bag together
Pin both pieces of the bag together with
the ears in position. Cut a piece of ribbon
for the strap and pin it in place too. Sew
around the edge with running stitch.

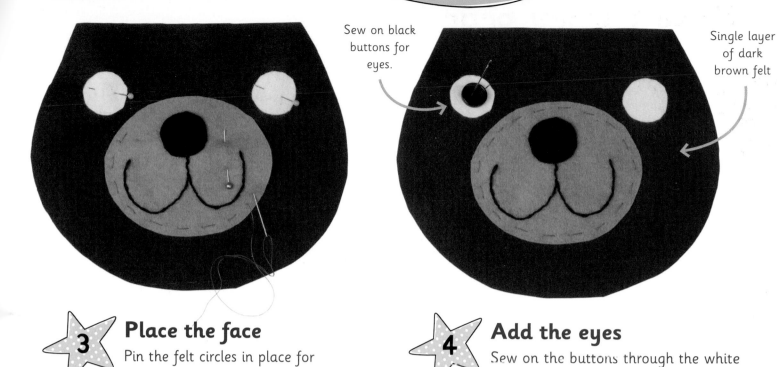

Sew on black buttons for eyes.

Single layer of dark brown felt

3 Place the face

Pin the felt circles in place for eyes. Pin and sew the muzzle to the head with running stitch.

4 Add the eyes

Sew on the buttons through the white circles of felt on the front of the head.

Make Percy panda or Clara koala

Percy and Clara are made in a similar way to Barney. Just use different felt shapes for the eyes, nose, and ears, and use backstitch to make a mouth.

47

Butterfly clips

Butterflies can really brighten up old hair clips.
Why not make them as lovely gifts for your friends?

For a pretty effect, sew **running stitch** in a different colour thread around the edge.

Put a smaller shape on top of a larger one then **sew** them to a piece of braid along the centre.

Add pretty decorations such as felt shapes.

Headbands
Another way to use these butterflies is to attach them to a **headband**.

Add detail with pearly buttons and braids.

You will need

thin paper • felt • scissors • needle
• sewing threads • braid or ribbon
• tapestry needle and embroidery
thread • glue • hair clips

48

1 **Make the templates**
Trace the templates on page 58 onto paper, then pin them onto felt and cut them out.

2 **Sew on decorations**
Using a different coloured thread, sew on felt shapes as decorations.

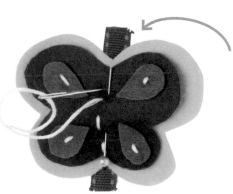

Cut ribbon or braid to the length of the clip.

Cut the antenna to the length that you want.

3 **Assemble the butterfly**
Place the smaller shape on the larger one, then pin it to a piece of braid or ribbon. Sew together using running stitch.

4 **Add the antennae**
At the top, push a threaded needle in then out, bringing the thread with it. Tie a knot in each end and trim off the extra thread.

Press down firmly.

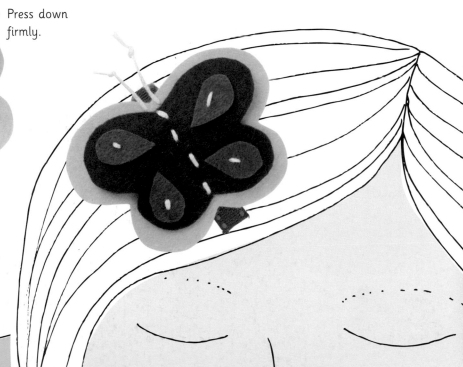

Apply the glue.

5 **Attach to hair clip**
Spread glue onto a hair clip and press it firmly onto the back of the ribbon. Allow to dry.

They're off!

They're under starter's orders. Which hobby horse will you ride to win the race? Will it be Checky, Red, or Blue Rocket?

Top tip

You can make the **manes** from wool, string, or trimmings used for curtains or lampshades.

We're almost neck and neck! Giddy-up!

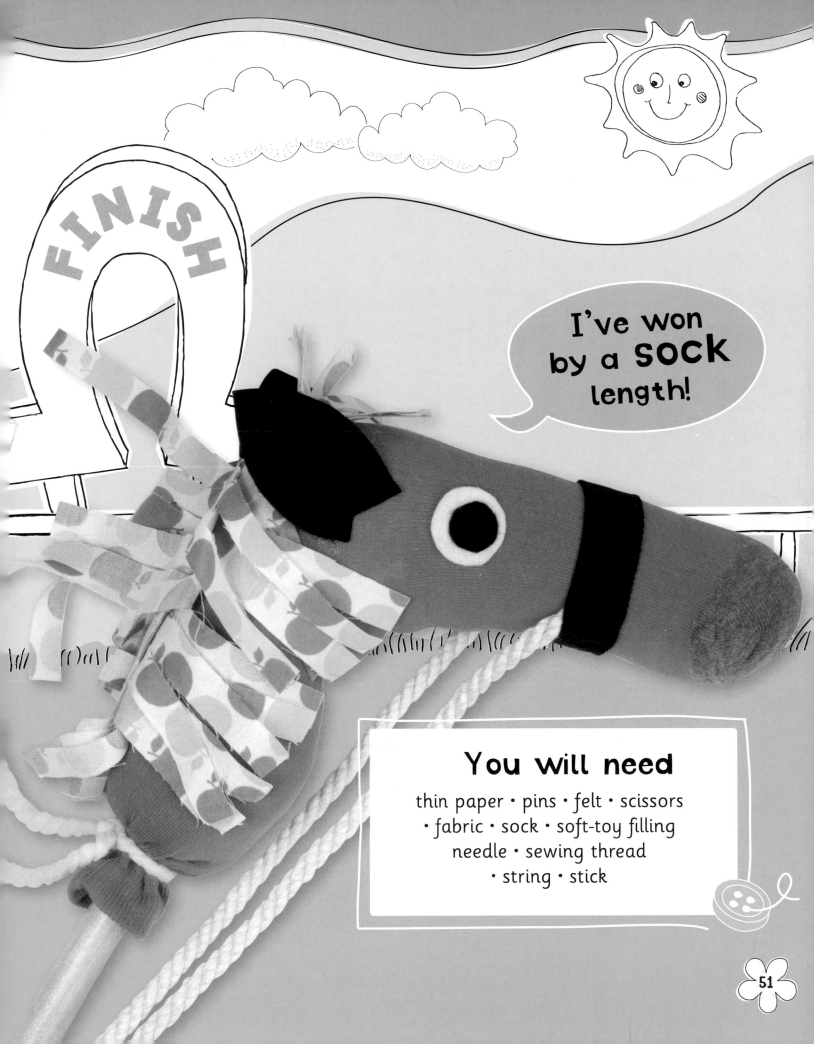

I've won by a **SOCK** length!

You will need

thin paper • pins • felt • scissors • fabric • sock • soft-toy filling needle • sewing thread • string • stick

51

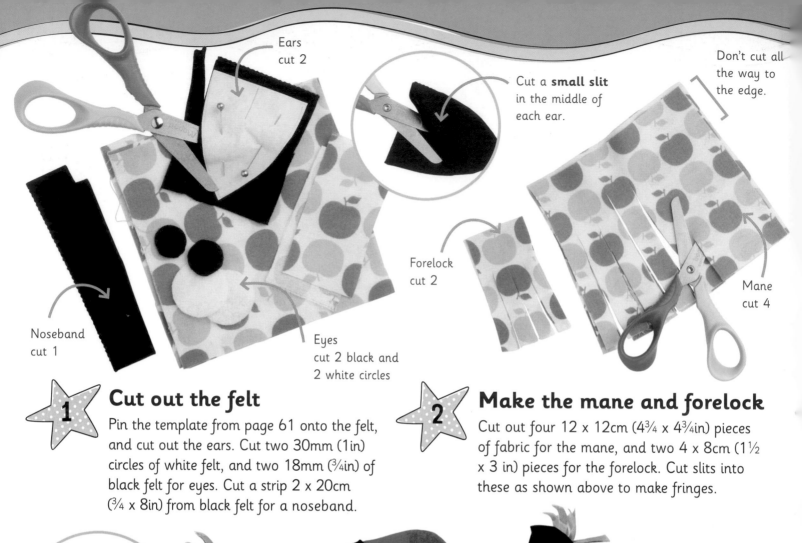

Ears
cut 2

Cut a **small slit**
in the middle of
each ear.

Don't cut all
the way to
the edge.

Forelock
cut 2

Mane
cut 4

Noseband
cut 1

Eyes
cut 2 black and
2 white circles

⭐ 1 Cut out the felt

Pin the template from page 61 onto the felt,
and cut out the ears. Cut two 30mm (1in)
circles of white felt, and two 18mm (¾in) of
black felt for eyes. Cut a strip 2 x 20cm
(¾ x 8in) from black felt for a noseband.

⭐ 2 Make the mane and forelock

Cut out four 12 x 12cm (4¾ x 4¾in) pieces
of fabric for the mane, and two 4 x 8cm (1½
x 3 in) pieces for the forelock. Cut slits into
these as shown above to make fringes.

Sew on the
2 pieces
of felt for
the eyes.

Sew several **extra
stitches** on top of
each other to give
extra strength to
the reins.

⭐ 5 Sew on the ears and eyes

Sew on white and black circles for
the eyes on either side of the head.
Then stitch on the ears.

⭐ 6 Sew on the reins and noseband

Cut a length of string for reins. Tuck
the ends of the reins into each side of
the noseband. Pin in place, then sew.

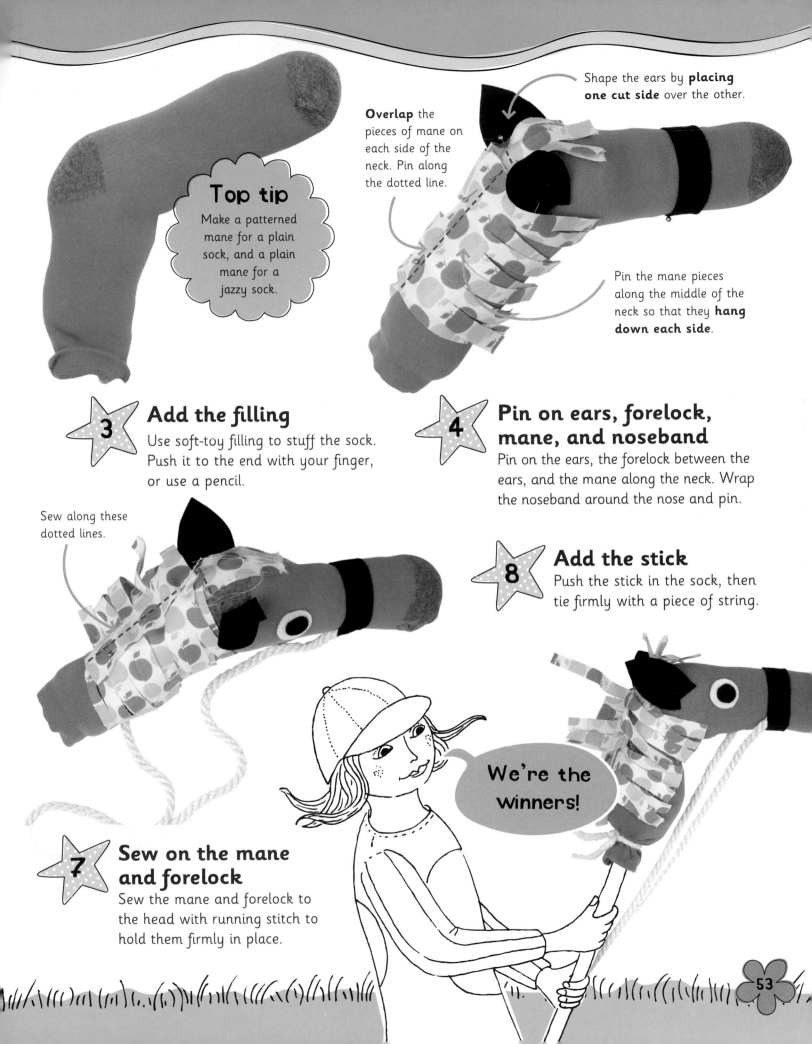

Top tip

Make a patterned mane for a plain sock, and a plain mane for a jazzy sock.

Overlap the pieces of mane on each side of the neck. Pin along the dotted line.

Shape the ears by **placing one cut side** over the other.

Pin the mane pieces along the middle of the neck so that they **hang down each side**.

3 Add the filling

Use soft-toy filling to stuff the sock. Push it to the end with your finger, or use a pencil.

4 Pin on ears, forelock, mane, and noseband

Pin on the ears, the forelock between the ears, and the mane along the neck. Wrap the noseband around the nose and pin.

Sew along these dotted lines.

8 Add the stick

Push the stick in the sock, then tie firmly with a piece of string.

7 Sew on the mane and forelock

Sew the mane and forelock to the head with running stitch to hold them firmly in place.

We're the winners!

Why make ordinary **bookmarks** when you can sew **fancy** ones?

Use **stretchy hair bands** to make your bookmarks.

You can use **rickrack braid** instead of ribbon.

Create your own style

Mix and match your favourite colours of **ribbon, button,** and flower for your bookmark.

You will need

patterned cotton fabric • scissors
• needle and sewing thread
• buttons • ribbon • rickrack braid
• elastic hair bands

Fancy bookmarks

You'll never lose your place with these clever ribbon bookmarks. Just sew a pretty button onto a fabric flower, add a ribbon, and you're done.

Gift idea
Why not give your friends who like to read a lovely personal bookmark?

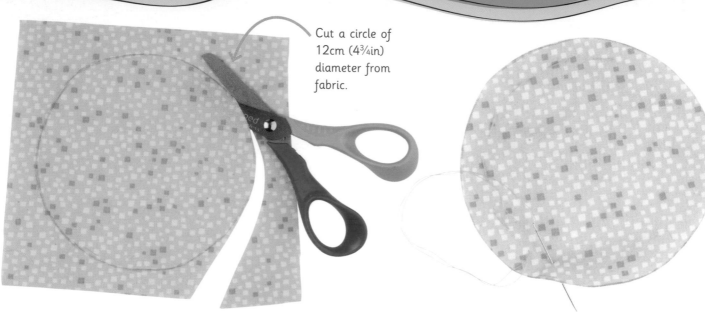

Cut a circle of 12cm (4¾in) diameter from fabric.

 1 ## Cut out the fabric
Draw a circle on a piece of fabric, then carefully cut it out with scissors.

 2 ## Sew around the edge
Sew long running stitches all the way around the edge of the circle.

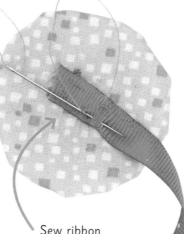

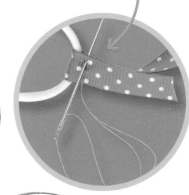

Sew ribbon around **elastic hair band.**

Sew ribbon onto the **back** of the rosette.

 5 ## Add a button
Sew on a button in the middle of the gathers.

 6 ## Sew on the ribbon
Sew the ribbon to the back of the rosette. Measure the ribbon's length by wrapping it around your book. Cut, then sew the other end of the ribbon around the hair band.

Pull together then squash down.

Sew a **few stitches** to hold everything down.

Pull the thread
Take one end of the thread and pull tightly to gather the edge together.

Flatten the sewn edge
Press the gathers down then hold them in place with some stitches.

Top tip
Measure your bookmark by **wrapping the ribbon around your book** before you sew on the hair band.

Don't lose your place! Bookmark it!

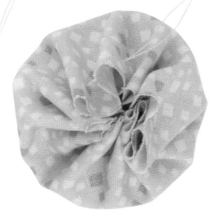

Templates

Use these handy templates to cut out fabric shapes.
You'll need them to make the projects in this book.

How to make a template

 Draw the templates
Place thin paper over each template as
shown here. Then trace over the lines.

 Cut out the templates
Carefully cut around your drawn shapes
then follow the instructions for the project.

Bunting heart

from page 22

Butterfly clips

from page 48

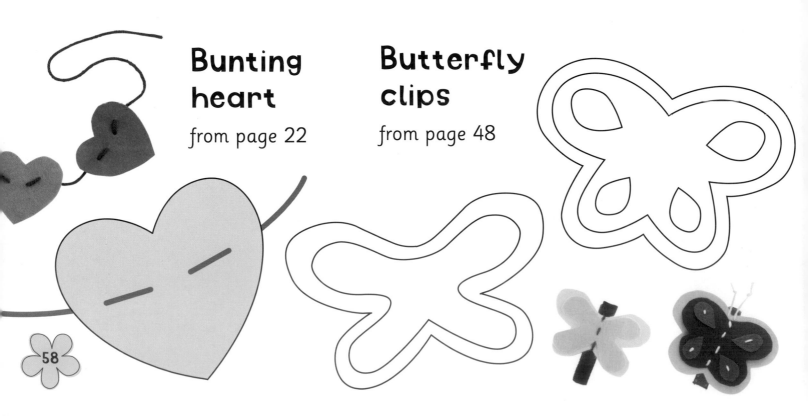

Sewing cards
shapes from page 16

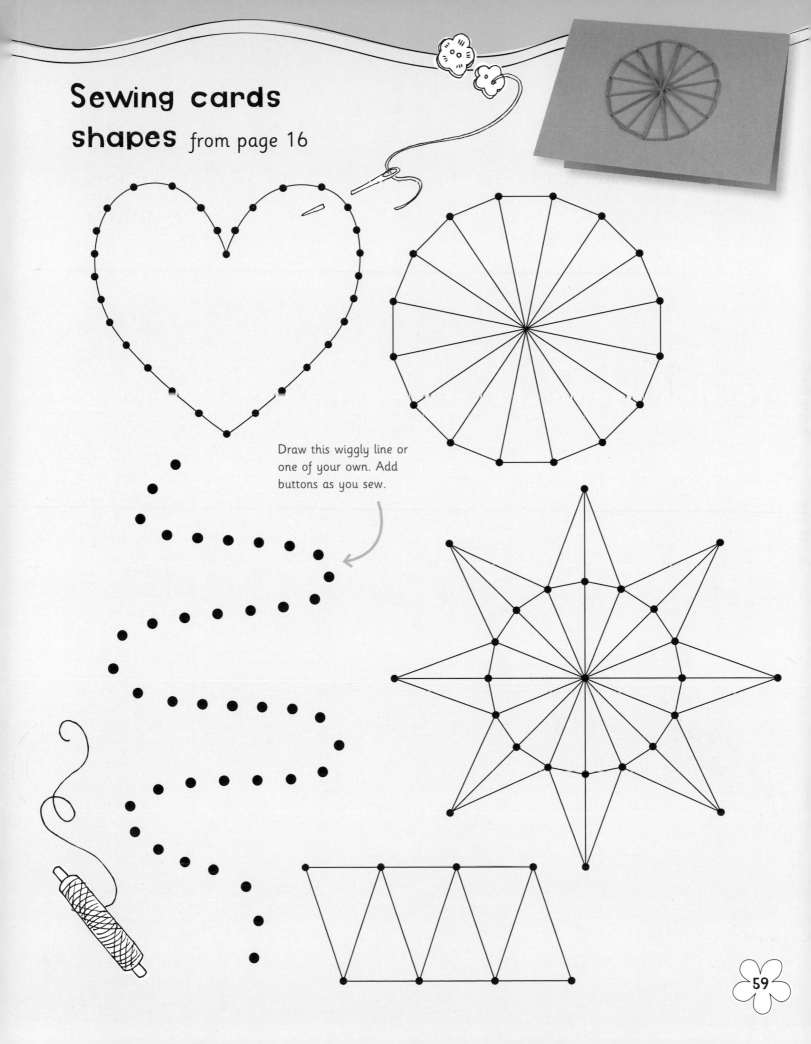

Draw this wiggly line or one of your own. Add buttons as you sew.

Rainbow birdies

from page 28

Tail

Body

FOLD

Beak

Wings

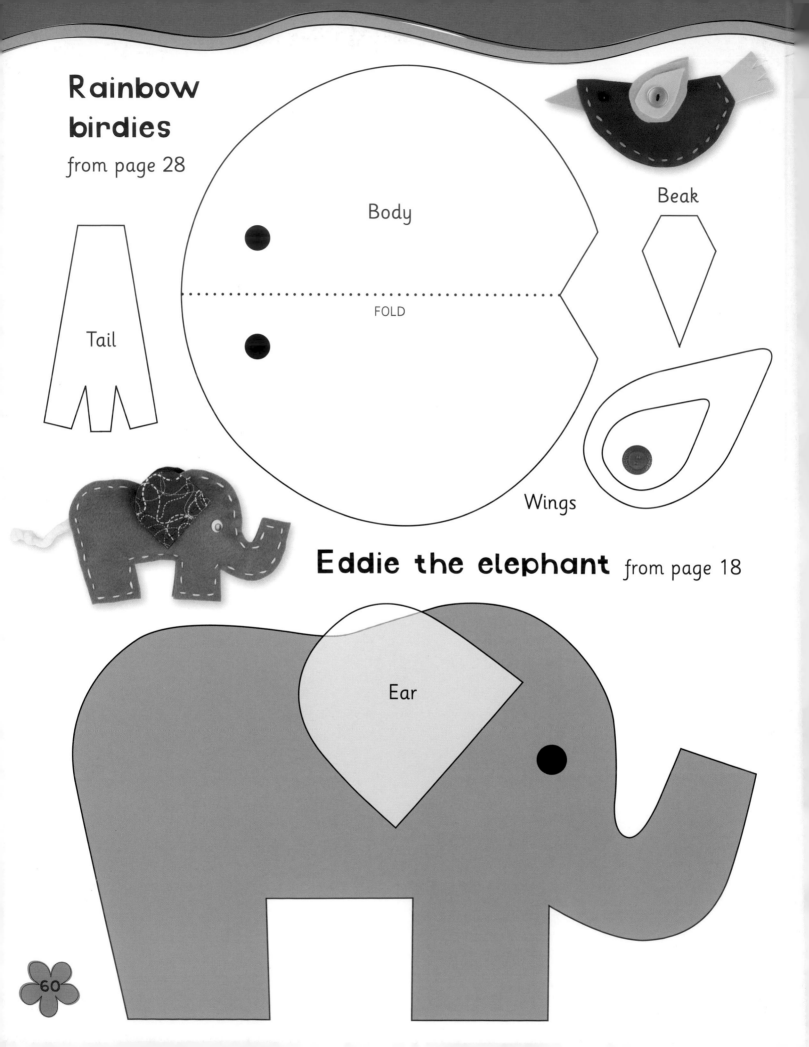

Eddie the elephant from page 18

Ear

60

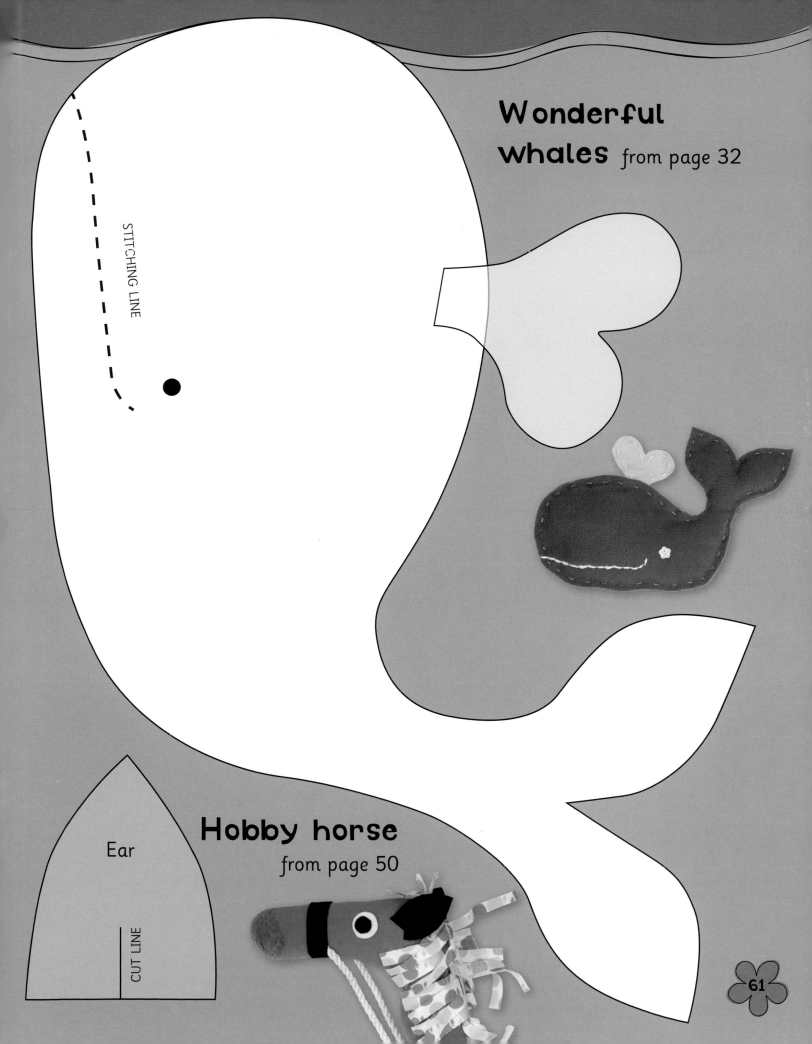

STITCHING LINE

Wonderful
whales from page 32

Ear

CUT LINE

Hobby horse

from page 50

61

Fat fish

Jellyfish

Under the sea

from page 40

Thin fish

Starfish

Bottle carrier
flower from page 24

62

Barney bear bag

from page 44

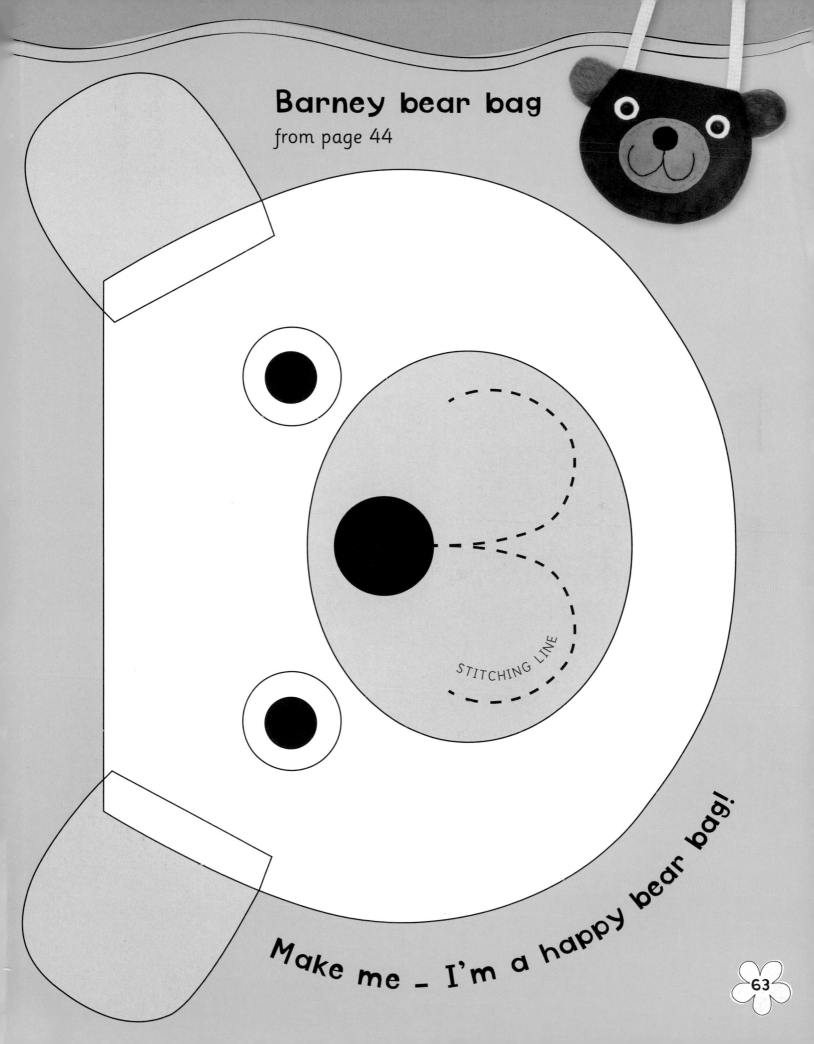

STITCHING LINE

Make me – I'm a happy bear bag!

Index

Acknowledgements

With thanks to Laura Palosuo for proofreading, and James Mitchem for additional editing.

With special thanks to Hannah Moore for creating and making the projects, and to our hand models Eleanor Moore-Smith and Annie-Mae Lane.

Tidy up!
When you've **finished sewing,** put everything away, and if you think you've dropped pins or needles, you can use a magnet to help you find them!